MIKE CRIPPS

TURNING
PENS
AND DESK ACCESSORIES

Schiffer Publishing Ltd®

4880 Lower Valley Road, Atglen, PA 19310 USA

DEDICATION

TO HOBBY WOOD TURNERS EVERYWHERE.

Designed by Audrey L. Whiteside

ISBN: 0-7643-0051-2
Printed in China

Library of Congress Cataloging-in Publication Data

Cripps, Mike
Turning pens and other items/Mike Cripps; text written with and photography by Jeffrey B. Snyder.
p. cm.
ISBN 0-7643-0051-2 (paper)
1. Turning 2. Pens 3. Writing -Materials and instruments. I. Snyder, Jeffrey B. II. Title
TT201.C74   1996
684'.083--dc20   96-13550
                CIP

This book is meant only for personal home use and recreation.It is not intended for commercial applications or manufacturing purposes.

Published by Schiffer Publishing Ltd.
4880 Lower Valley Road
Atglen, PA 19310
Phone: (610) 593-1777; Fax: (610) 593-2002
E-mail: Schifferbk@aol.com
Please visit our web site catalog at
www.schifferbooks.com

This book may be purchased from the publisher.
Include $3.95 for shipping. Please try your bookstore first.
We are always looking for people to write books on new and related subjects. If you have an idea for a book please contact us at the above address.
You may write for a free catalog.

In Europe, Schiffer books are distributed by
Bushwood Books
6 Marksbury Avenue
Kew Gardens
Surrey TW9 4JF England
Phone: 44 (0) 20-8392-8585; Fax: 44 (0) 20-8392-9876
E-mail: Bushwd@aol.com
Free postage in the UK. Europe: air mail at cost.

ACKNOWLEDGMENTS

I would like to thank Wood Craft for supplying pen kits and accessories for this book. They may be reached at Wood Craft, 210 Wood County Industrial Park, P.O. Box 1686, Parkesburg, West Virginia 26102-1686. Toll free phone number: 1-800-225-1153; fax: 1-304-428-8271.

CONTENTS

ABOUT THIS BOOK --- 4

COMMON SENSE INFORMATION --------------------- 5

GENERAL INFORMATION --------------------------------- 8

TURNING PENS --- 17

GALLERY -- 57

SUPPLIERS -- 64

FOREWORD

I have known Mike Cripps for many years and it is a particular pleasure to introduce him to you as the author of this book. He is a big hearted, jovial and highly talented turner who is particularly suited to lead you through the techniques he describes.

Mike and I first met at one of his early wood turning meetings held at a local Cricket Club. His enthusiasm for turning and willingness to help others encouraged a lot of members to improve technique and try other projects.

About a year later, after a lot of hard work, Mike became one of the founder members of the A.W.G.B. (The Association of Woodturners of Great Britain) which was launched in 1987 at the first Loughborough seminar.

In 1990, after being made redundant, Mike decided to set up his own turning school/wood and tool store. This has been a great success and hundreds of aspiring turners have passed through his classes, some now winning competitions, a tribute to Mike's teaching skills and encouragement.

The project in this book is good practice for any turner — just follow Mike's superb instructions and enjoy your turning.

Mac Kemp
Chairman
Middlesex Wood turners Association

ABOUT THIS BOOK — TURNING PENS AND OTHER ITEMS

Fifty years ago, when the fountain pen reigned supreme, it was expensive, a much valued gift, and very personal to the owner. Since that time, the arrival of the inexpensive, mass produced ball point writing implement has removed the individuality from a pen. Today, it is commonplace to have a selection of pens on the desk for anyone to use. However, the arrival of the hand-made, individual wooden pen has made it once more a personal and treasured possession. It is a happy marriage of modern technology and the craftsman's skill. Pens made in good grade, highly figured hardwoods are a joy to behold and make wonderful presents.

Pens may be given individual characteristics to suit the users' requirements: substantial pens for the desk, compact ones for wallets or purses, stubby pens for those who prefer them, or delicate pens for those with a light touch.

Some of the items in this book are made from kits which are available from your turning supplier. These include fountain pens, twist pens (retractable ball-point pens), roller ball pens, and click pencils. Perfume applicators and paper knives are also made using similar kits. Pens may be given character by including styles which reflect the owners interests — such as baseball bat pens or pens with golf club clips.

Accurate drilling, careful gluing, and delicate wood turning to fine tolerances followed by finishing techniques are the stages that I will take you through in this book. A gallery of photographs of pens made by English wood turners is included to stimulate your ideas for design and form, and assist you in producing items of which you will be proud.

COMMON SENSE INFORMATION FOR BEGINNERS TO WOOD TURNING

OBTAINING KNOWLEDGE

Before turning wood on your own, make the effort to watch someone else doing it and do not be afraid to ask questions. Most people that I have met who work in wood are friendly and are usually only too pleased to help someone starting in this rewarding hobby. Books and videos are, of course, a great way of obtaining knowledge of the subject; however, the best ways to learn are either to take a 'Beginner's Course' or get some hands on experience if you can.

BUYING YOUR FIRST WOODLATHE

I am often asked, "Which lathe should I buy?" My answer is always "Get the best that you can afford." Cheap imported lathes very often are noisy, this being caused by inferior electric motors that vibrate excessively. This vibration reverberates through the drive belt to the lathe headstock, which is usually clad in a thin, rattly casing. This vibration can be reduced by easing the tension on the belt slightly and making sure all bolts and screws, including the bench securing bolts are tight. It is well worth the effort to check them over before using the machine.

Whether you buy new or second-hand, when looking for a reliable machine the following points are worth your consideration:

(a) has it got a heavy steel plate or cast head?
(b) are the head and tailstock spindles hollow to allow the use of standard fittings (1 or 2 morse tapers)? This will save money as you will be able to buy 'off the shelf' lathe accessories.
(c) place a drive centre in the headstock and a centre in the tailstock and check for alignment with the points. If they do not meet properly you will always drill oversized holes and have excess vibration.
(d) place a mandrel or large accessory such as a drill chuck in the headstock and check for sideways movement. If the lathe has standard bearings, movement denotes a worn bearing. If, however, bearings are tapered roller types this could be cured by adjustment.

(e) check for side play in the tailstock where it located on the bed. If badly worn, this will cause you to drill inaccurately and will cause vibration.
(f) make sure that the tool rest locks on the bed and in its support securely and without excess force on the securing levers. REMEMBER that you frequently move the tool rest.
(g) if buying second-hand, take a mental calculation of the chucks and accessories that come with it, usually it is the presence of these that makes a used lathe an attractive proposition as a new wood turning chuck can cost around $150 to $200. A drill chuck and live centres cost around $50 and drives and mandrels $20 to $30 each when purchased new.
(h) smell the motor to check for any burnt smells which denote it is already burnt out or on the way. Also, disconnect the belt and see if it runs quietly. A noisy motor usually means the bearings on the shaft need replacing.

BASIC TURNING TOOLS

The ROUGHING GOUGE, as the name implies, is used for roughing down square to round. It is also used for the preliminary shaping work on spindle turning e.g. shallow curves and tapers. I find that it is an excellent tool for flat areas when face plate turning as well.

A 3/4" roughing gouge is the ideal tool to start with. The approach to the wood should be as follows. Place the roughing gouge firmly on the tool rest with the blade pointing upwards. Lower the tip of the tool down slowly until the bevel rubs on the wood without the cutting edge coming into contact with the wood (this is what I call the no-cut position). Continue to lower the cutting edge down onto the wood until you obtain the first sign of a shaving. Only when this is obtained should you travel along the tool rest from left to right and vice versa to true up the wood between centres.

The PARTING TOOL is an essential tool. I would suggest that a 1/8" wide parting tool is the best to start with and will be the cheapest for spindle turning. The parting tool is used to make incisions into the wood at each end of a piece to provide a waste end which is discarded when the piece is parted off the lathe.

This tool can be used in two ways but when making deep parting cuts or grooves, always ensure that you make the cuts slightly wider than the tool so that it does not get gripped. One method is pointing the tool upwards while sitting it firmly on the tool rest and pushing it in an upward direction. A second method is to start with the tool again sitting on the rest and slowly levering the tip downwards using the tool rest as a fulcrum. NEVER go below the level position and point the tool downwards as it could be pulled in towards the wood and jammed against the tool rest.

The parting tool is also useful for rolling beads and cutting recesses for chucks on faceplate work. If the parting tool is used on its side, flat on the tool rest, the point can be used for scoring decorative grooves in the wood using this scraping cut.

SPINDLE GOUGES come in a range of sizes from 1/8" to 3/4". Most commonly today they are made from round section bar but traditional or continental gouges are still being produced. These are made from pre-formed curved section steel.

The main uses for the spindle gouges are for forming beads and coves, rounding over and squaring up end grain. I would suggest a 3/8" is a good one to start with.

When cutting coves or hollows, point the centre of the gouge at the starting point, cutting down one side to just past the centre of the bottom of the cove and then repeat the process on the other side. By cutting down the hill, or from the largest toward the smallest diameter, you will be compressing together the fibres in the wood with the bevel while the cutting edge does its job. This will give you a good finish. Cutting uphill separates the fibres and leaves an inferior finish. REMEMBER, if you slowly swing the end of the handle in a circular motion, the shape of the cove will also have a round profile. To cut beads or balls, the tool has to be rolled over working again from the top toward the bottom with the bevel rubbing.

The SKEW CHISEL is probably the tool that takes a fair bit of practice before it is mastered. I would suggest that you purchase a 1" OVAL SKEW as this is a size that is good for planing and making beads and squaring ends. An oval skew is nicer to handle than a rectangular section skew as the corners tend to stick on any nicks or grooves in the tool rest.

To plane a cylinder to a smooth finish, raise the tool rest to centre height and position it as close as possible to the pre-roughed out cylinder. Place your thumb firmly on the tool rest just past the end of the wood and tuck the skew between the thumb and the tool rest. Now, using the short corner of the skew and not using any more than 1/8" from the point, the tool should be about 45 degrees to the wood. Obtain a shaving and travel along the tool rest. You may have to alter the angle of the tool or raise or lower the blade slightly. REMEMBER the shaving is the reward and the sign that you are cutting correctly. You will be able to cut coming back along the tool rest by holding the tool at the same angle.

To form beads with the skew I prefer to use the long point and as when cutting only use the actual point and up to 1/8" from it. NEVER cut uphill. Start at the top of the bead, rolling the skew over as it cuts through 90 degrees with the blade vertical on completion of the cut at the base of the bead. When making beads or spheres, work on the right then the left, repeating the process and bringing on both sides together. REMEMBER when cutting over beads etc., rub the bevel all the way — lifting the handle up as the cutting action goes down.

The BOWL GOUGE, as the name implies, is the tool for turning bowls. A 3/8" high speed gouge made from 1/2" round steel with a long and strong handle is the best size to buy. I maintain a bevel of approximately 45 degrees and remove the sharp corners the makers provide by grinding two long blades on the top of the gouge.

Although I love to use the bowl gouge for spindle turning, particularly for long flowing curves for goblets and vases, its main use is for bowls and facework. It is important to constantly rub the bevel to support and steady the cutting edge around external and internal curves. Cutting with the tip unsupported by the bevel makes it 'grabby' and prone to digging in.

To find the right position, lay the bevel on the wood (making sure the tool is firmly on the tool rest) so that you are in the 'no cut' position. With the bevel in contact with the rotating wood, slowly raise the handle until a shaving appears. Stay with it and guide it along or round the surface of the object you are making. You will soon appreciate the supported feeling that the bevel provides as the gouge tip cuts. REMEMBER, if you are changing the shape of the wood from a square corner to a curve, it is much easier if you cut away the corner to a wide chamfer first. To cut wood without the bevel rubbing is like driving a car without wheels!

All the tools that I have just written about are cutting tools which are usually used in an upward mode with the SKEW chisel being the exception as by raising the tool rest it is usually used mainly with the toolrest in the 'level with centre' position.

I would strongly recommend that you buy good quality tools. For the tools we have discussed so far — ROUGHING GOUGE, PARTING TOOL, SKEW CHISEL, SPINDLE GOUGE and BOWL GOUGE — I feel that it is worth the extra cost to purchase high speed steel. Tools of high speed steel will hold their edge up to five times longer and will not be affected like carbon steel by overheating from the electric grindstone.

The last of the basic tools to talk about are SCRAPERS, which are mainly used to remove any bumps and ridges left after using the Bowl Gouge. A scraper is used in a downward position with the tool rest set back from the work to give room to use it at this angle. When sharpened correctly a sharp burr of metal stands up proud on the end of the tool which will produce plenty of shavings.

I have found that carbon steel scrapers, which are less expensive than high speed steel, work extremely well. The burr can be raised by pressing a hard metal bar across the end of the scraper which forces the cutting edge burr upwards (this is known as using a ticketer).

Scrapers can be made in different shapes. For faceplate work a square ended scraper, say 1" to 1 1/4" across with the corners relieved to allow the movement of the tool from the centre to the edge of flat surfaces and vice versa, is ideal. By grinding the corners back slightly, snagging is avoided when in use. For inside bowls and open vessels a 1" to 1 1/4" ROUND NOSED SCRAPER is ideal. The metal should be as sturdy as possible to avoid vibration when cantilevering inside a bowl on the tool rest.

SHARPENING THE TOOLS

The SKEW CHISEL and the PARTING TOOL only need re-grinding occasionally and honing with a slipstone is all that is required but keep them sharp at all times. A slipstone made from metal impregnated with diamond dust is an effective way of sharpening them.

I sharpen the end of the ROUGHING GOUGE to a shallow bevel of approximately 45 degree - REMEMBER, although useful for turning softwood etc. long bevels are more grabby for beginners to use. Be very careful to keep the blade straight across by rolling the tool over on the grinding wheel from one corner to the other. A common fault with new turners is only to sharpen the rounded part of the cutting edge which, if done for several sharpenings, forms two long points like cats ears on the gouge.

I sharpen the SPINDLE GOUGE to a finger nail shape with a bevel angle of somewhere between 45 degrees to 60 degrees. If you hold the gouge upwards and rotate it on the grindstone from left to right you will very quickly form a sharp point on the Spindle Gouge and lose the rounded profile. To avoid this rotate the tool, sharpening from centre to right following the existing finger nail shape. You will find that in doing this when you start (with the handle straight and in line with the grindwheel) when you finish the handle will be approximately 45 degrees to the right of you. Now repeat this process from the centre to the left. ALWAYS use only light pressure — only a small touch on the stone is required. It is a good idea to practice this manoeuvre with the grinder switched off first.

The BOWL GOUGE is sharpened in much the same way but if you want the cut back profile I use on my bowl gouges, start from the middle and, following the edge of the tip profile, roll the gouge right over so the flute is facing the wheel, pushing it upwards. Then, to sharpen the cutback section, sharpen as before going toward the other side.

I always use SCRAPERS with the manufacturer's name uppermost so I know which way to use it; however, when sharpening these tools on the grindstone, I turn them upside down. Because the stone is rotating toward you and downwards, it naturally forms a good burr on the bottom edge of the tool which, of course, becomes the top when you use it.

Your grindstone should be kept at a sensible height so that you can use it without stooping. Mine is about 4' from the ground. It is a great help to have an anglepoise light on the stone. The following safety tips should be observed:

(1) NEVER use a grinder without eye protection e.g. visor, goggles or safety glasses. I find that those little clear plastic windows that are provided very soon get scratched and become impossible to see through.

(2) NEVER work on a grindstone that is clogged or out of true. Diamond Wheel Trimmers are much less expensive now and they clean the stone and trim it in just a couple of passes. REMEMBER a clean stone cuts cooler and sharpens efficiently. Take precautions by wearing a mask when trimming the stone as a large amount of dangerous dust is created when this is done.

(3) NEVER ever use your grindstone on soft or non ferrous metals such as copper or brass. If the stone is clogged with this type of material it can overheat with use and even shatter.

An alternative method for sharpening tools now being sold by a major British tool maker consists of wooden discs mounted on an arbor with aluminium oxide abrasives adhered to them. These can be held in a chuck on the lathe and you can clearly see what you are doing. The recommended speed is around 1400 r.p.m on a 5" disc.

USING THE LATHE
SPINDLE TURNING (OR TURNING BETWEEN CENTRES)

As a general rule I prefer to turn small diameter work (say up to 2" x 2") at a fairly fast speed. If you are reducing square stock to round, this makes the task quicker and avoids excess vibration being transferred through the tool to the joints in your hand.

Let us assume you have a piece of square timber mounted securely between centres. Select a speed of around 1200 to 1500 r.p.m. If we look at the pulleys contained within the headstock when selecting our turning speed, it is important to note that the smaller the size of the pulley, the faster the speed of the lathe will be. Put on your visor or safety goggles — ALWAYS PROTECT YOUR EYES.

Always avoid inhaling wood dust when sanding. Use a mask and an extraction unit. An airstream helmet is good but will not prevent a build up of fine dust in your workshop.

To mount the wood between centres when I am teaching, I use a ring centre or friction drive as opposed to a 2 or 4-prong drive. This method is safer because if you have a 'dig in' the wood will stop rotating and slip on the centres. A pronged drive keeps on going regardless and a heavy 'dig in' will result in chunks of wood flying off or the whole piece leaving the lathe. If you do not possess a friction drive, reduce the tension on the drive belt. This will also provide a safety mechanism.

Adjust your tool rest to around 1/2" below centre. Rotate the wood by hand before switching on to make sure it clears the tool rest. Then check all securing levers or nuts including the headstock swivel (applicable on rotating head lathes only) — the tool rest support to the lathe bed — the tailstock to the lathe bed and finally the securing lever to the quill of the tailstock.

Using a 3/4" or 1" Roughing Gouge, point the cutting edge upwards away from the rotating wood onto the tool rest. NOTE — NEVER place any turning tool onto the wood unless the tool is firmly on the tool rest first. Now, gently lower the tip of the gouge until the bevel (flat area next to the cutting edge) is rubbing on the rotating wood without cutting. As lightly as possible (I call this the no-cut position), and still with the gouge on the rest, lift the back hand up and look for the finest of shavings. Use only light pressure toward the wood and obtain a light buzz from the cutting edge as you ease the tool along the tool rest and back.

Stand in nice and close to the lathe with your feet apart and use body movement to move the tool from left to right and vice versa. REMEMBER, outstretched arms are wobbly things. Keep the inside part of your arm against your side and move the tool along with body movement only. As soon as a gap of, say, no more than 1/2" appears between the tool rest and the wood, stop the lathe and move the tool rest in as close as you can while checking that the wood rotates freely without rubbing on the tool rest.

Switch on and, while looking at the horizon (top edge of the wood), make a nice smooth cylinder. Do not allow the tool to swing — this will give you a bad shape. Obtain a shaving, keep the tool at this angle, and move along the tool rest.

GENERAL INFORMATION ON THE LATHE AND WOODTURNING TOOLS

A ring centre, seen in place here on the lathe, is the best centre for beginners. It is most forgiving if you have a dig in.

Mark the centre of the blank with a small hole made with an awl. On softer woods, tighten up the tail stock until the drive centre grips. For a harder piece of wood, we might have to tap the centre with a hammer to begin to drive it into the wood.

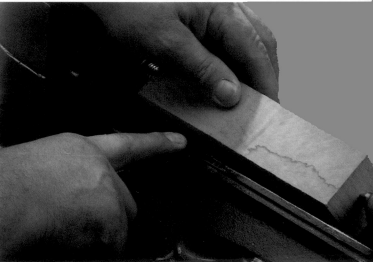

The smaller the pulley on the headstock, the faster the work is going to go.

Before you turn on the lathe, rotate the wood by hand to make sure that it is not hitting the tool rest. The top of the tool rest should be positioned approximately 3/4" below the centre. This height will vary according to the diameter of the timber, the height of the lathe, and the comfortable working postion the turner wishes to adopt.

Double check all of the locking handles to the tail stock, and the tool rest, making sure they are tight. This precaution will help you avoid accidents. If your lathe is of the swivel head type, make sure the swivel nut is tightened as well. Otherwise, the head could turn while the wood is spinning.

The tool should be kept straight across at its cutting edge. I will explain this in detail later when we cover tool sharpening.

THE ROUGHING GOUGE:

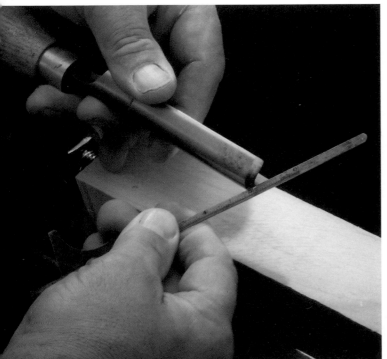

Begin with the tool in the "no cut" position.

Let's look at the tools now. The first of the tools is the roughing gouge. For people first learning to turn, the roughing gouge is much easier to use if the bevel edge is kept short, approximately at 45 degrees. Longer bevels may be preferred as a turner become more experienced. But in the hands of someone new to wood turning, a long bevel is both grabby and more difficult to use.

Raise your arm, lifting the handle until the blade just touches the wood and begins to form shavings.

Remember, the slower you go, the nicer the finish, half of the rifling has been removed in this picture.

Slowly move along the length of the wood. Only light pressure is required with a sharp tool. As you move along the wood, roughing the corners off, all you should hear is a light buzz. That is the sign that you are doing the job correctly, making a nice spray of shavings as you go. Keep the tool firmly on the tool rest. Ensure that the bevel of the tool is always rubbing against the wood, this stablizes the tool for you and makes it safer to handle as well as your tools will not need to be sharpened as often. Someone new to wood turning tends to stand a long way out from the lathe and work with arms extended, this tends to make the tool vibrate and wobble, making it hard to get a nice finish. Move in close. Keep your lower arm (the one holding the lower part of the handle) resting against your body, using your body to move the tool back and forth.

If you travel too fast, rifling will occur. Spiral grooves are created all along the wood.

The roughing gouge is mainly used to reduce square stock to round and for truing up unbalanced timber. However, the roughing gouge is also a useful tool for shaping shallow curves and hollows. Always work down the hill (from the largest to the smallest diameter). By doing this, you are compressing the fibers of the wood together and cutting the wood as it likes to be cut; cutting uphill will separate the wood fibers and give you an inferior finish.

A good parting tool to start turning with is a 1/8" parting tool. Later on, you may feel like investing in a diamond profile 3/16" parting tool (seen on the left) which moves more easily through the wood, without a tendency to be gripped. The diamond profile is, of course, also a much stronger tool for deeper cuts.

While parting the wood, never allow the tool to fall below the centreline position because it can be pulled in by the rotating wood and get caught between the wood and the tool rest.

The approach to the wood, as before, is from a high position with the bevel rubbing. Lift the handle upwards and lower the cutting edge gently down onto the surface of the wood. Continue cutting into it, then go back to the starting position again and take a second cut alongside the first to widen the groove. This will prevent your tool being grabbed in a narrow parting cut. The first use of this tool is to remove the scrap wood from either end of the piece. There are two reasons for doing this. One is to remove the marks left by the drive and live centres and the other is to ensure that the wood is cut away on the end of the piece of timber. This area is often full of small hair cracks where it has dried.

The second method of using the parting tool is with it sitting firmly on the tool rest, the bevel rubbing, pushing upwards only. Again widen the groove as before to keep the tool from getting gripped.

Cut down the diameter of the waste wood so that it is a little larger than the lathe centres. This will keep the waste wood out of our way, giving us better access to the ends of the wood.

Then move to the left to round the other side. Remember, always look at the horizon to obtain the best view of the shapes you are making.

The parting tool has one other useful function. Placed on its side, flat on the tool rest in a downward scraping mode, it is excellent for making fine decorative lines and grooves.

The parting tool is also very useful for forming beads. The wider the parting tool, the easier it is to use for this function. Make two shallow grooves, one on either side of the proposed bead. Place the parting tool with the bevel rubbing in the centre of the bead-to-be and, with a rolling action, roll over to the right two or three times until you have rounded over the square corner on the right.

THE SPINDLE GOUGE:

With the parting tool, we can further enhance the appearance of the cove by cutting two small shoulders, one on either side. This gives the cove a classical look often found in beautiful and period furniture.

THE SKEW CHISEL:

Raise the tool rest to the lathe centre height or just above centre to use the skew chisel.

The spindle gouge is used for generally shaping wood, forming coves and beads, and can be used to clean up end grain. The best spindle gouge for beginners is the 3/8". To make a cove, start with the bevel rubbing, supporting the cutting edge, and swing the handle in a perfect circular motion. If the handle travels in a circle, your cove will be round. Smooth flowing actions are the secret of nice shapes.

I would suggest you buy a 1" oval skew chisel. You will find this tool much nicer to handle and much smoother to run along the tool rest than the old style square edged skew chisel. The square corners tend to catch in all the marks in the tool rest. The oval chisel glides across them.

Use the short corner of the skew for planing the wood. We are only going to use the area 1/8" from the short corner. Do not cut with the higher part of the blade.

The skew chisel is used for rounding over ends, forming balls and beads. To round the end you must rub the bevel along the edge of the wood.

First put your thumb slightly to the right of the starting position on the tool rest. Lay the bevel of the tool on, raise a shaving just above the short corner.

Slide the tool along the tool rest in a planing action. If the tool judders and doesn't run smoothly, either raise or lower your back hand slightly or change the angle of your cut very slightly. When you feel it is right, continue with the planing action.

Using the skew chisel to make beads.

I am using the skew chisel to make a ball. Work first to the right and then to the left, bringing the ball into shape on both sides equally.

THE ROUND NOSED SCRAPER:

Buy a 1" or 1 1/4" round nosed scraper manufactured from good, sturdy metal. The scraper doesn't have to be made of high speed steel. The round nosed scraper, used in the downward angle, is ideal for cleaning up, removing tool marks, smoothing down troublesome end grain, and is invaluable when face plate or bowl turning.

THE BOWL GOUGE:

A 3/8" bowl gouge is a good size to start with in your tool kit. You can see how large this is.

SHARPENING THE TOOLS USING AN ELECTRIC GRINDING WHEEL:

Sharpening the roughing gouge. Make sure the top is straight across.

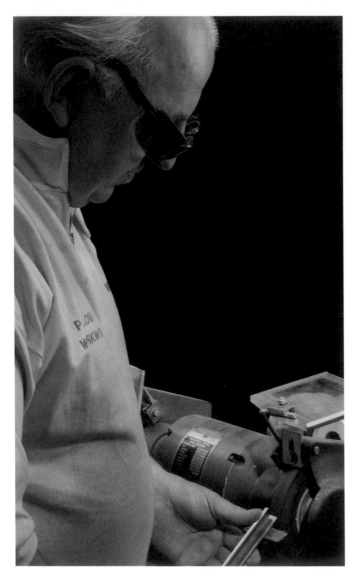

It is essential that your grindstone is fixed at a sensible height where you can view what you are doing without stooping. Standard work bench height is far too low for most people. The grindstone should also be well lit. Light is an essential aid when examining a tool for sharpness; a blunt section of the blade will reflect light and a sharp section will not. I prefer not to use the manufacturer's see-through shields. I find they soon become scuffed and marked and are very difficult to see through. Always wear safety goggles or glasses while working on the grindstone. This is very important. Always ensure that your grinding wheel is running true and that it is clean. Both of these functions can be achieved with the use of a diamond (or other form of) trimmer.

Sharpening the spindle gouge. Refer to the notes in the general material for further sharpening details.

TURNING PENS

MAKING PENS, AND OTHER OBJECTS FOR THE DESK:

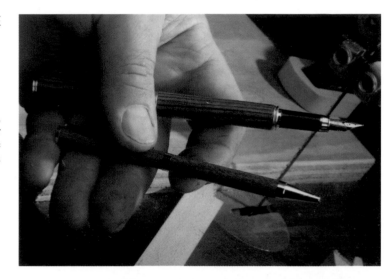

There are many varieties of pen kits, pencil kits, fountain pen kits, magnifying glasses, letter openers, and perfume pens available in your local or mail order wood store. These objects are great fun to make and are wonderful gifts for your friends and family. For those of you who turn for profit, these can be a nice source of income as well.

Most of these kits are made on the same principle, requiring careful preparation of the wood blank, accurate drilling and sanding, and a very delicate approach to the wood turning and finishing. As you can see, the wood veneer is extremely thin; this veneer can be less than 1/32 of an inch thick. This thickness is predetermined by the bands and the size of the actual pen components. As you can see from the photograph showing the end section of a tube surrounded in wood, it is extremely thin. It is for this reason that we have to be careful to set up our equipment accurately in order to achieve good results.

This picture shows a pen partially assembled, illustrating for you that it is indeed the size of the dividing band which determines the finished diameter of the wood surround.

Let's look at the equipment necessary for making pens, which many of you will already have in your shop. First of all, there is the band saw. Use a square to ensure your blade is cutting at 90 degrees to the table of your bandsaw.

This is the drilling jig I use when making pens.

Adjust your fence (I'm using a wooden fence here). I use one of my push sticks as a thickness gauge for setting up the fence to ensure that the prepared pen blank, when it is cut, slides nicely into my jig. The jig is used for the drilling operation. (See the next picture.)

The wood fits into the jig as shown.

NEVER EVER saw wood on a bandsaw unless you use push sticks as I have shown here, one stick to push and one stick to hold the wood against the fence. There is no need to put your hands near the bandsaw blade.

Make up a push block as shown here. The push block will give you another safe way to cut the wood. It also makes a useful gauge for determining the length required for the pen blanks. Have the guard on the saw set a little way above the height of the wood so that it doesn't obstruct your vision. Never have too much of the saw blade exposed for obvious safety reasons when you are using the saw.

On your drill press, lower the quill of the drill and hold a square against the drill bit you are going to use. Check the table alignment with the drill which should be 90 degrees. This operation is most important. If it is not done the drill will pop out the side of your prepared pen blank, ruining it completely. (Practice on blanks cut from inexpensive wood or off cuts first.)

Here is a prepared pen blank (there are two of these needed to make most kits). Place the blank in the jig.

The top line is the actual length of the tube. Below it is another line approximately 1/8" away where we will cut the blank off after drilling.

Never ever cut your pen blanks exactly to size and allow the drill to come out the other end. As soon as the drill passes through the end, it splits the wood. This tip, leaving the waste wood on, will save you a lot of heart ache and destroyed pen blanks. Here is an overall shot of the drill press table.

Here is the mark showing you the depth we will drill to, which is beyond the length of the tube and not as far as the end of the pen blank.

Drilling the pen blank. Here is the drilling jig firmly clamped to the drill table. A drill vice clamped in position would also be a good method of holding your drilling jig in place. The block in front keeps the blank from moving sideways.

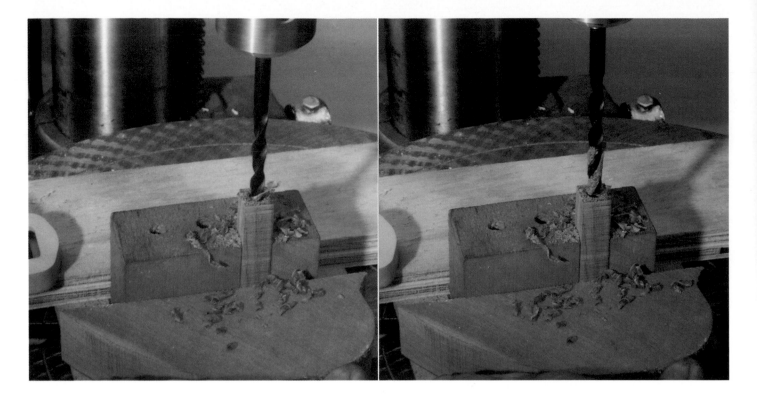

Drill the blank with the correct sized drill bit. It is most important that you drill only 1/2" in depth, pull the drill out to clear the swarf and repeat this process every half inch of the way. This will help you to avoid either splitting your blank and overheating your drill. Set the drill to a fairly slow speed, fast drilling of wood can lead to overheating and charring the inside of the hole and also cause splitting. Fast drilling can also make the hole oversized, resulting in a loose fit on your tubes. Always use a sharp drill bit.

This is the depth gauge of the drill. Set it to the depth required. Pen kits mainly come from the far east and your local dealer, when he orders his kits, has no control over the varying sizes of the tube dimensions and lengths that arrive from shipment to shipment. It is therefore most important that every time you go to use a pen kit you check your drill and tube sizes for both diameter and length. Remember that if you glue tubes in oversized holes which do not provide a snug fit, the thin veneer of wood that is left will invariably squash and catch on the gouge during the turning process.

Here are the pen blanks, cut to size following the drilling process. The off cuts of exotic timbers and resins, etc., used for making pens may be thrown in the tin and kept. Spend a nice day making beads with them some other time or glue them together to make multi-color pens.

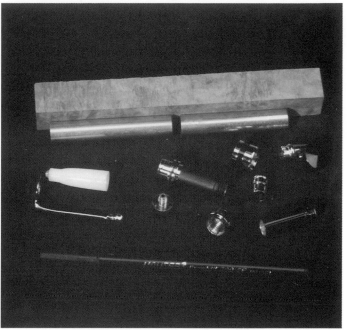

Parker style roller pen kit.

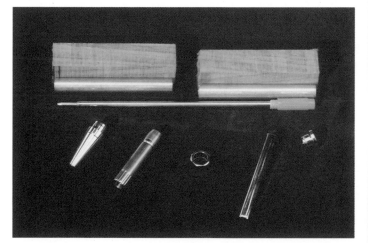

The component parts of a standard quality twist ball point pen kit.

Parker style twist ball pen kit.

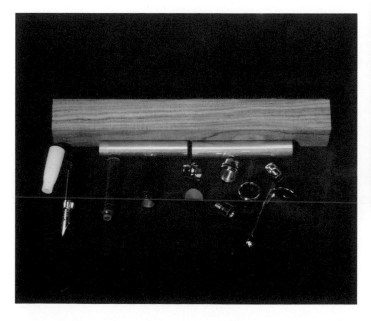

The components of a Parker style fountain pen kit.

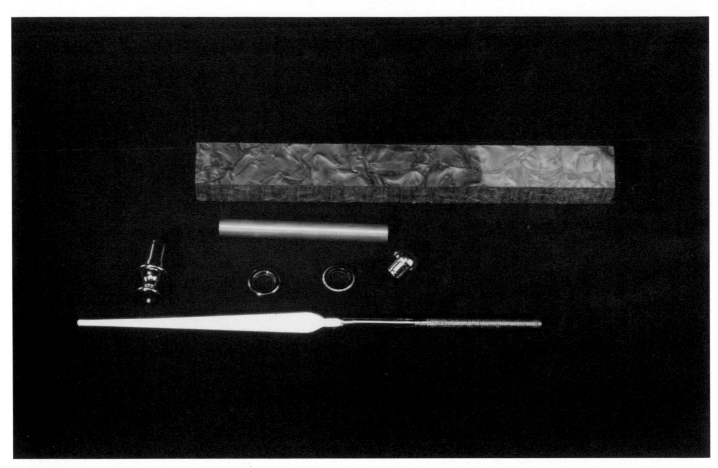

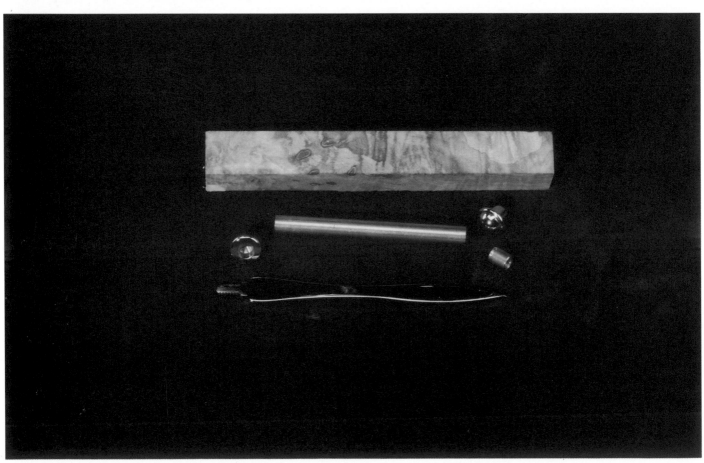

Letter opener kits.

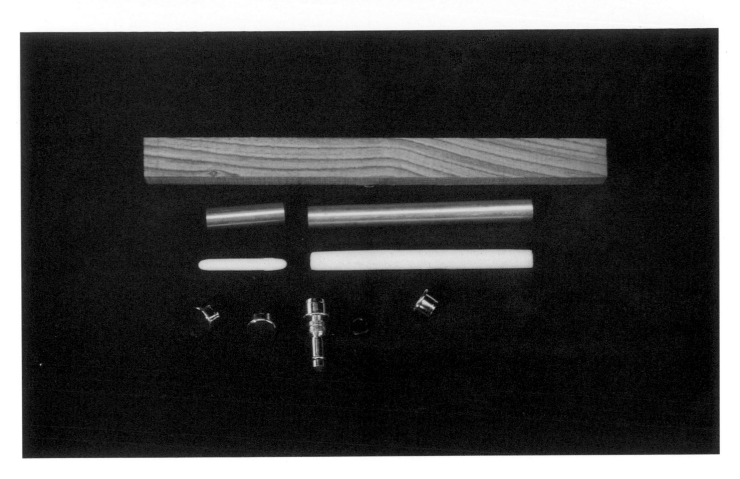

A perfume pen kit.

A magnifying glass kit.

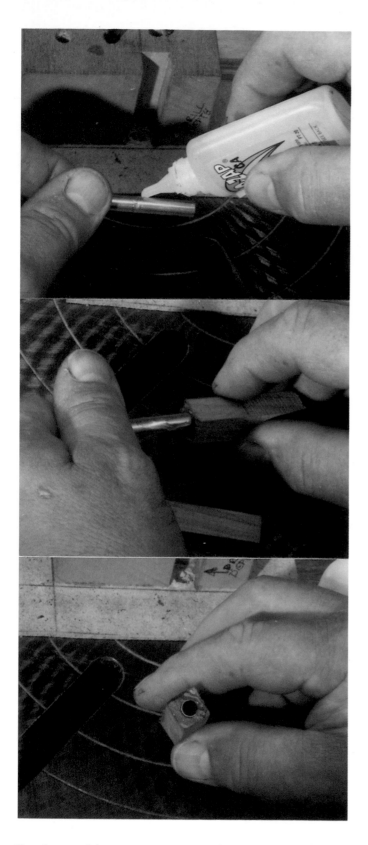

This picture shows me reaming out any surplus glue that may have crept down the inside of the tube and which would prevent the tube from sliding easily onto my pen turning mandrel.

Here I am applying a generous amount of cyanoacrylate glue to the brass tube. Push the tube in and out with a pumping action and revolve it as you push it down into the wood to spread the glue out evenly over the inner surface of the wood. The type of cyanoacrylate glue I am using is a slower setting one I feel more comfortable with as it allows more time to do the job. Some of these glues are so fast that the tube will stick, if you are not quick, half way into its position. Any glue that is recommended for adhereing wood to metal is suitable. If in doubt read the instructions on the container or ask your wood shop store owner.

When sanding, make sure that your fence is at 90 degrees to the sanding disk, using a square to align it.

Now check the table of the sanding machine, ensuring that it is also at 90 degrees to the disk.

The sanding machine is properly connected to the dust extractor. It is vital that you do not inhale wood dust. If you do not have an extractor, use masks for protection.

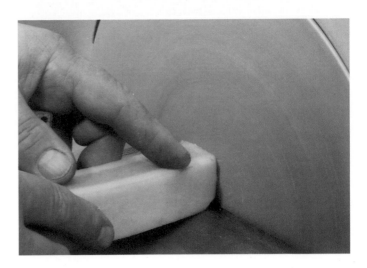

Here you see me cleaning the abrasive disk with a latex disk cleaner. The use of this implement will extend the life of your abrasives by at least ten times. Therefore, these make very good investments.

Squaring the ends of the pen blanks to a smooth finish on the sanding machine.

Viewing the ends to see that the wood is precisely level with the tubes. You will be able to tell that this is correct when you view the shiny ends of the tubes polished by the abrasive paper.

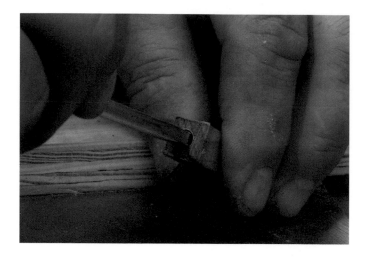

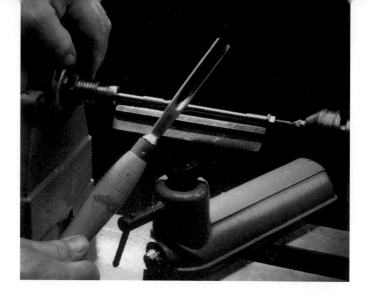

Remove any small burrs left on the ends of the tubes by the sanding operation to allow a good fit onto the ends of the pen mandrels.

I would also strongly recommend that you add to your small turning kit a small roughing gouge like the one shown here. This is a 1/2" #9 carving tool fitted to a small turning handle. It is the main tool that I use to make pens that are straight in design. The smaller tools are useful for making beads, coves, etc.

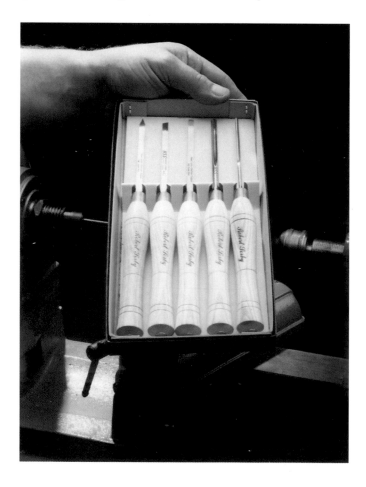

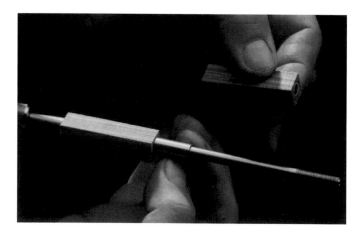

This is a pen mandrel which is available in a one or two morse taper to suit your particular lathe. [A list of suppliers can be found at the back of this book.] Various collars can be purchased to suit the variety of tube diameters which slide on the mandrel.

This is an ideal set of suitable good quality tools for making small objects such as pens, magnifying glasses, bobbins, etc. From left to right it consists of a 1/16" parting tool, 1/4" skew chisel, 1/4" round nosed scraper, 1/4" gouge, and a 1/8" gouge.

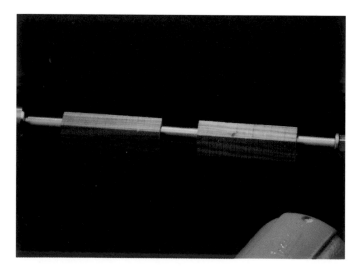

Between each piece of 1/2" square wood we have fitted a spacer which also serves as a sizing piece to enable you to get the correct dimension.

Pens and other small objects are best turned at the highest speed your lathe can give you.

Sand the wood smooth. Start off with fine grade P240 abrasive strips and move up to P600 on some materials.

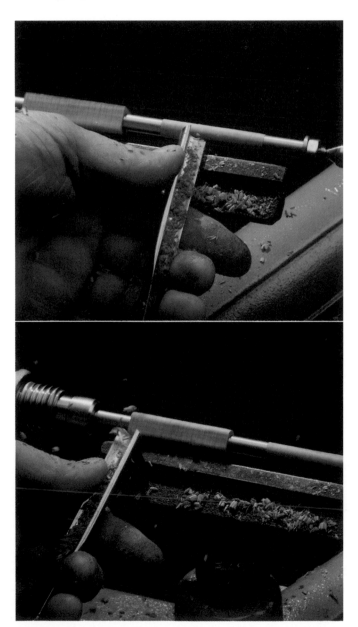

Turn the wood to shape with the roughing gouge. This is tulip wood.

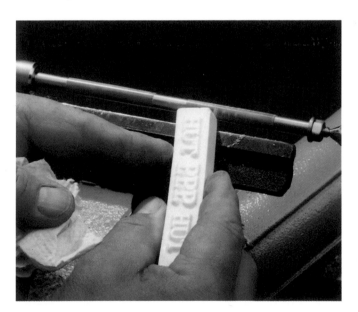

After sanding, burnish the wood with shavings held in your hand. Apply a two stage bar polish to the wood shafts. An alternative form of polish is a liquid friction polish which is brushed on and polished with a piece of rag. Using the stick polish, apply the brown (Stage 1) first, just a light smear across the wood. Then polish with a piece of soft paper or a small cloth. Turn the paper or cloth to a clean area and continue buffing it. Repeat the operation using the white (Stage 2) polish. If you have achieved a good finish prior to applying the polish you will have a brilliant shine.

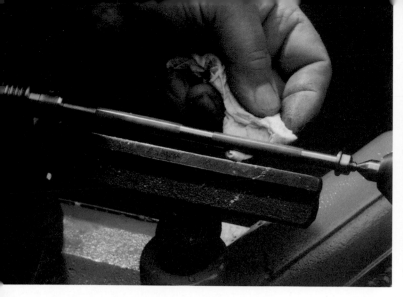

Buff the wood with a paper towel or a soft cloth.

Turn the gouge over to get into tight corners.

These are the larger mandrel bushes which suit the larger diameter components of the perfume pen. This is a piece of Kingwood, 3/4" square. The tubes on this particular kit are two different lengths.

Both tubes are rounded.

The first tube is turned.

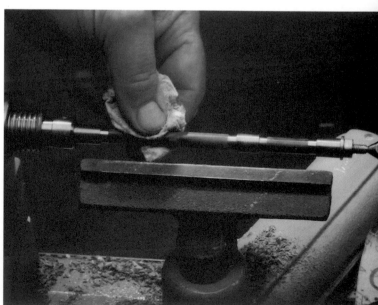

Buffing the first coat of bar polish.

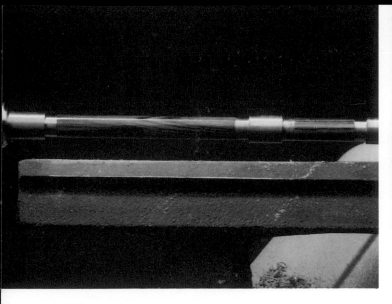

Kingwood has beautiful grain.

Rounding the handle with the 1/2" roughing gouge.

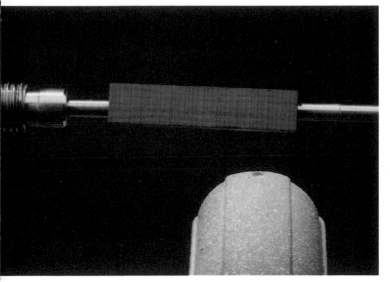

I will make a magnifying glass handle in Coca Bola.

I have turned this handle with a slight taper to give me an oversight of the balance of the shape I would like to make.

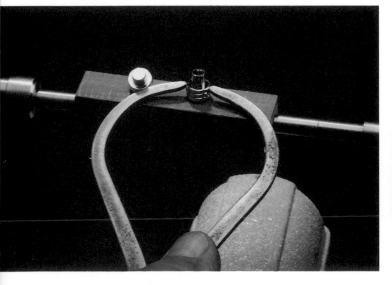

Because we are not restricted by bands in the middle as we are with the pens, we are able to make a more creative shape. These pieces are the end button and the holder for the magnifying glass itself.

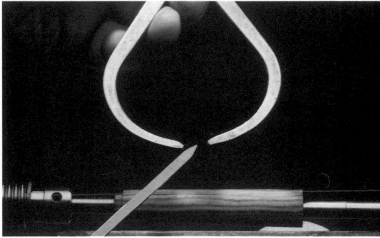

When you purchase calipers from the store they always come with very sharp points. This makes them very user unfriendly for wood turning and I would strongly recommend that you round them over as I have done with the pair shown here.

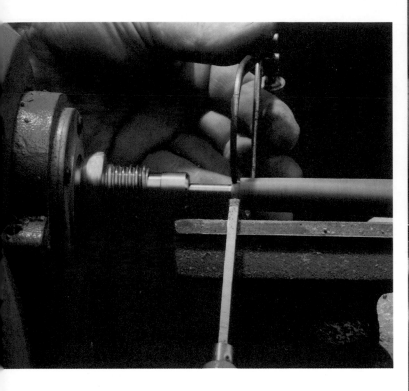

I have now turned a small collar to the size I have set on the calipers from the size of the fitting. I will also turn a bead and a hollow on the small end, intended to go next to the magnifying glass itself.

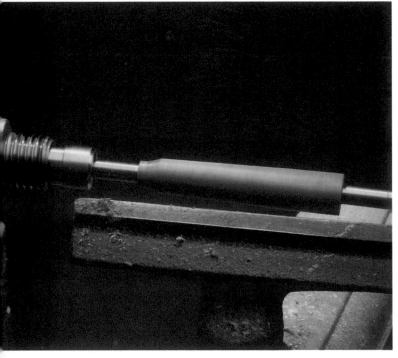

I have now formed a hollow from the edge of the intended bead down to the point I sized with the calipers. Round down the sharp edge with the roughing gouge.

Make a small bead at the back of the taper with the parting tool.

32

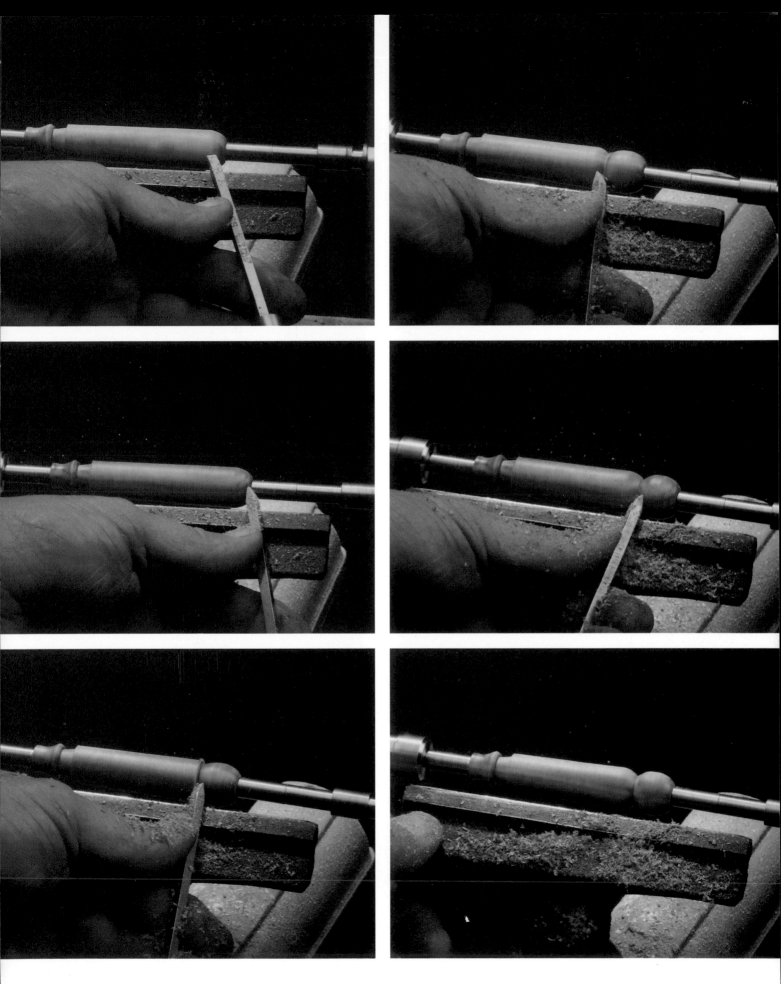

Form a ball and a half ball at the back of the tapered handle with the parting tool as shown.

Then add a long hollow sweeping down to just behind the bead at the top of the handle.

The handle is ready to sand and polish.

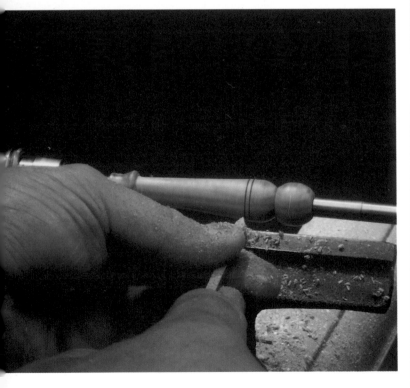

Add two small bands with the parting tool.

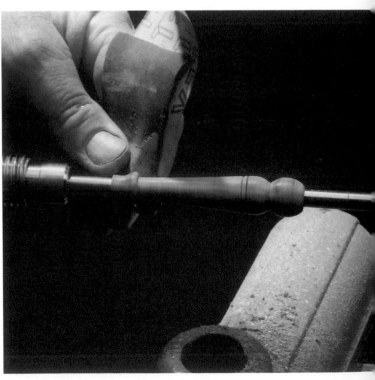

Sand the handle with the P240-320 and possibly up to P400 grade abrasive strips as before.

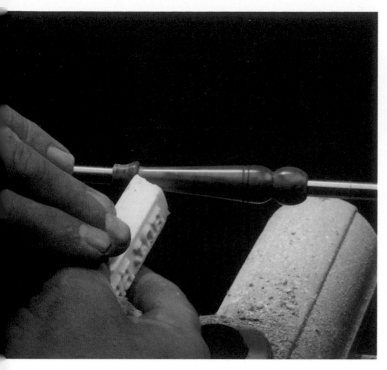

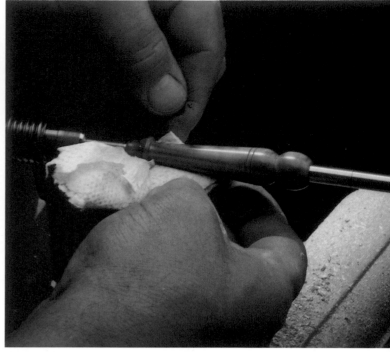

Apply both bar polish stages.

Buff with a paper towel or a soft cloth after each polishing stage.

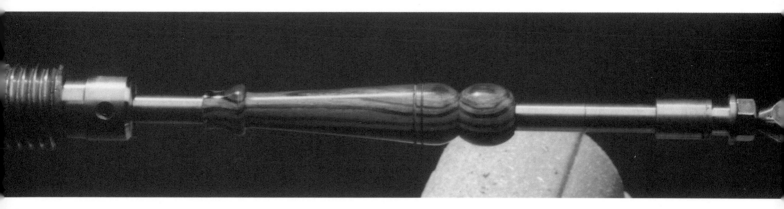

The polished handle.

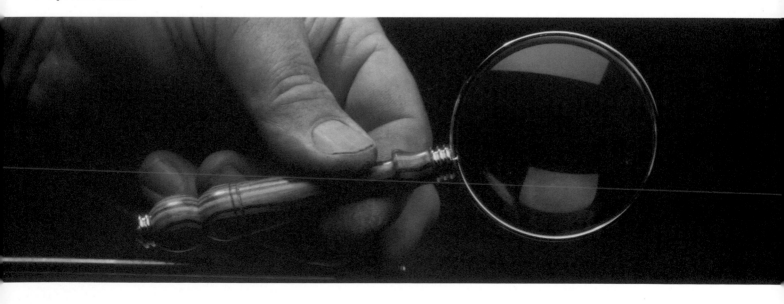

The assembled magnifying glass.

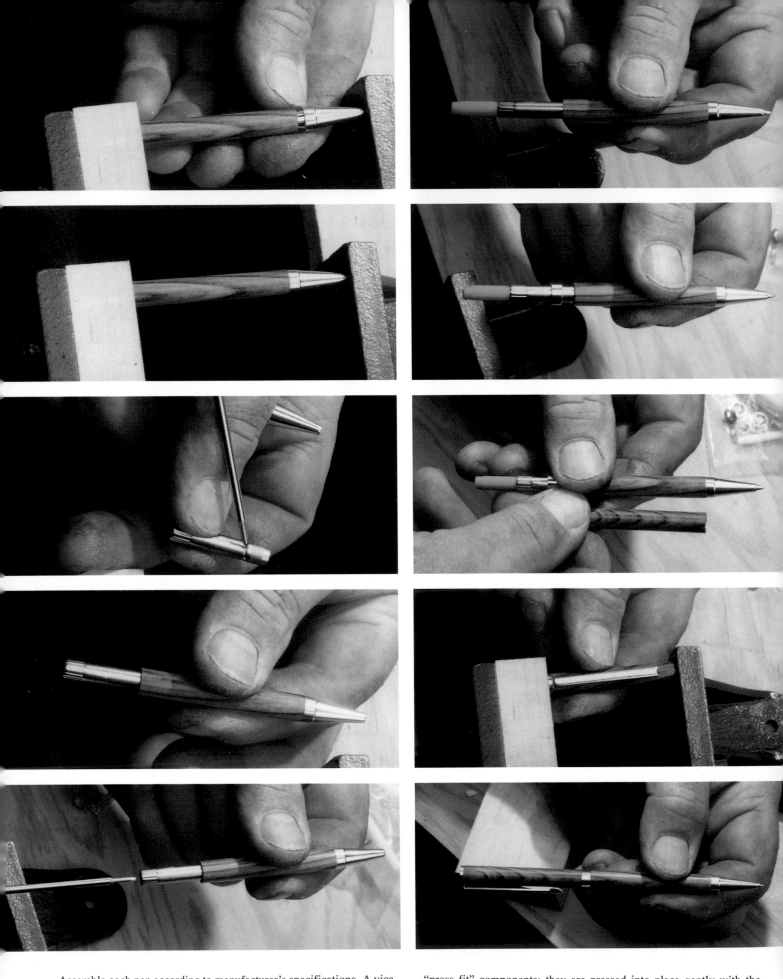

Assemble each pen according to manufacturer's specifications. A vice is the most important piece of equipment you will need. These are "press fit" components; they are pressed into place gently with the vice. This is the Parker style twist ball point pen.

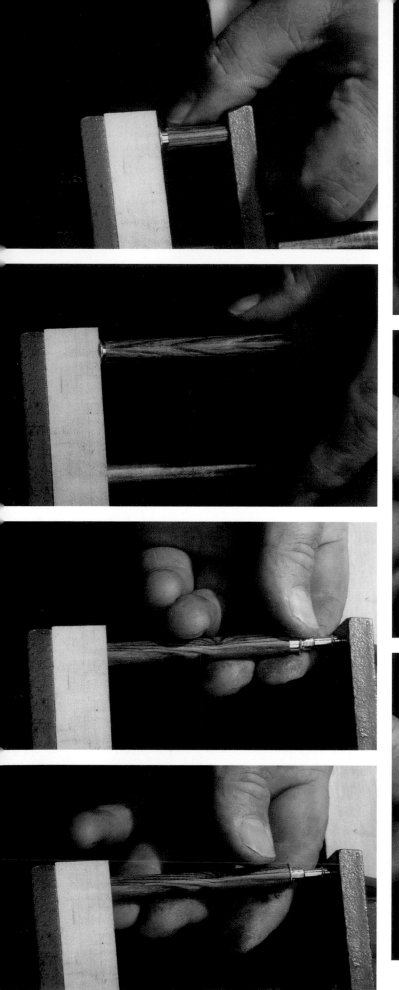

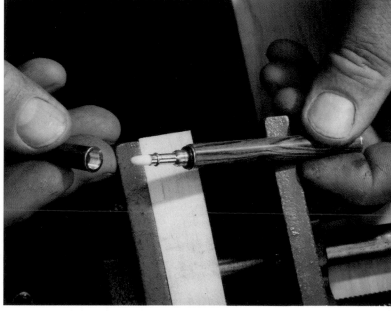

Press fitting together a pen-style perfume dispenser.

Some pens require a small niche cut into the shaft for the clip. A small rasp (file) is ideal for the job.

An array of pens and the magnifying glass. The pen at the bottom is a fountain pen. When making pens for women, it is best to leave the clips off. Ladies carry their pens in purses and do not require the pocket clip.

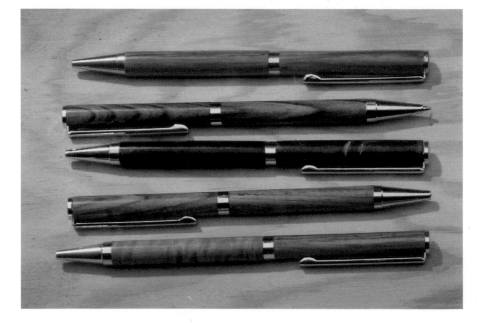

Assembled ball point pens.

These are fountain pen shafts of resin impregnated burr wood which will be used in the assembly of a Parker style fountain pen. Note the larger size of the fountain pen cylinders.

There was a natural imperfection in this resin which left this small hole.

One shaft is turned.

To repair the damage, first remove the cylinder from your mandrel and then apply some cyanacrylate glue to the chipped area. Don't leave the cylinder on the mandrel and get glue on the mandrel, you won't get it off.

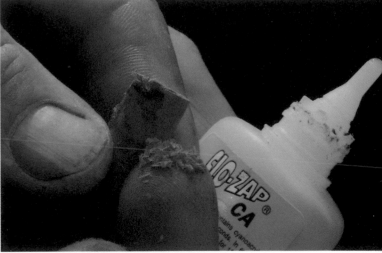

Turning the second shaft with my special 1/2" roughing gouge.

Add some dust of the same material to the glue.

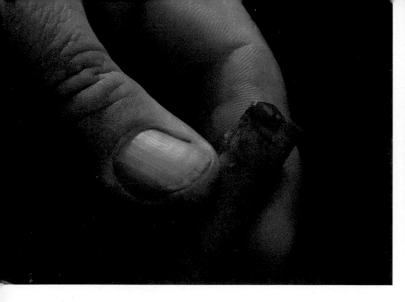

Add more glue over top of the dust and set the tube aside until it dries.

Sand the repair smooth with a fine grade abrasive strip.

The repair to the fountain pen cylinder has dried. Return the cylinder to the mandrel.

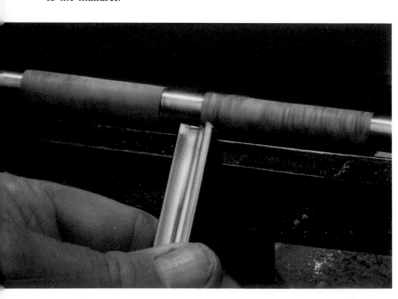

Smooth down the repair with the 1/2" roughing gouge. Make this a gentle approach with a sharp gouge.

The repair has been sanded, leaving only one small and acceptable chip along the edge. Polish and buff the cylinders as before.

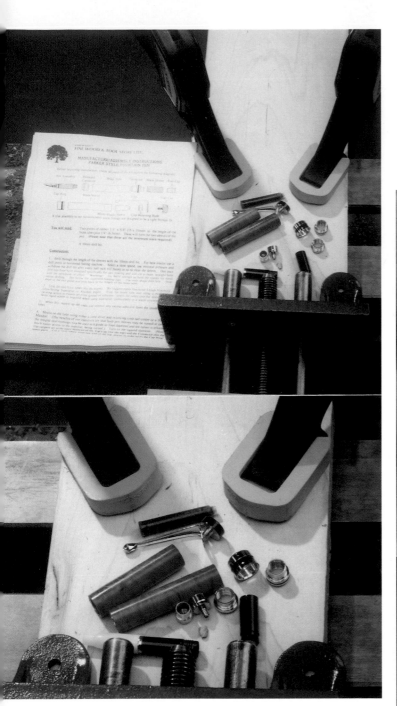

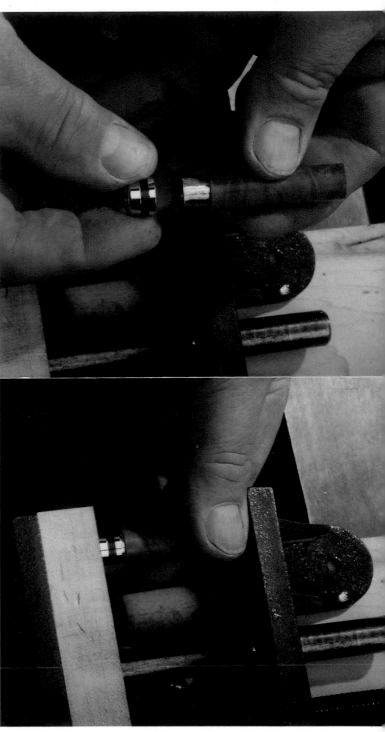

When assembling the Parker style fountain pen, there are two main fine points of assembly we must discuss. Both items are concerned with the top section of the pen.

The first item — part of the wood has to be turned away following the initial turning and polishing to house the decorative banding on the pen top. Note the rounded over end goes away from the wood.

The second item — I'll draw your attention to the top of the clip, which on this pen is flush fitting and does not require a groove.

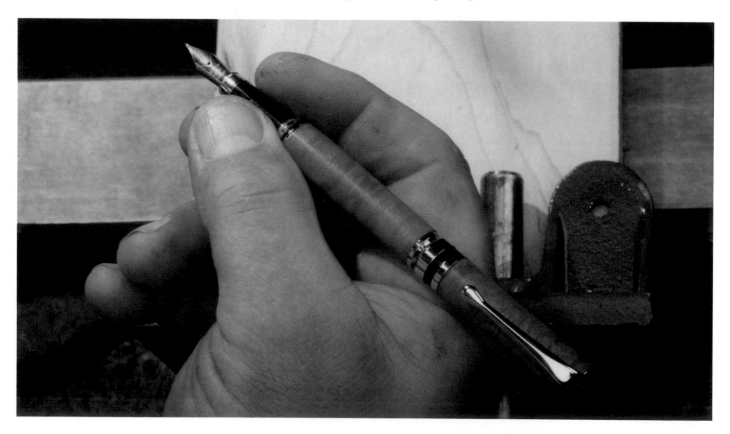

The completed Parker style fountain pen in resin impregnated burr wood.

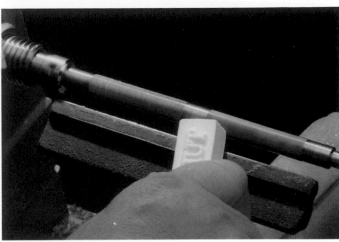

Next we'll turn fountain pen shafts in tulip wood. Wood cuts much faster than the resin we just finished turning.

Apply both coats of stick polish, buffing in between each coat with paper towel or a soft cloth.

Sanding the tulip wood. Keep moving the abrasive strip to avoid scratching the wood.

The right hand cylinder has been buffed to a shine.

Burnish the wood with shavings.

It is time to assemble the tulip wood fountain pen.

First assemble the bottom half of the tulip wood fountain pen. Press in the bush with the internal thread to receive the nib section.

On the other end of this piece, press in the similar bush to receive the long brass pen top.

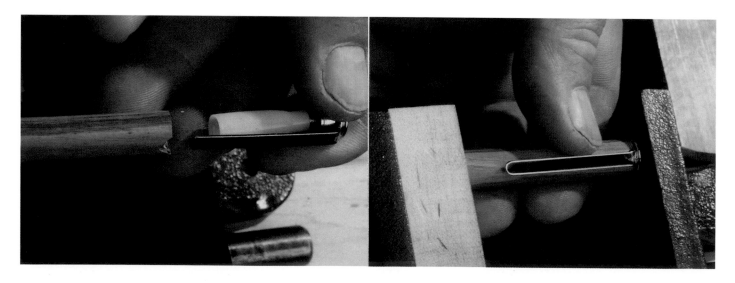

On the other half of the fountain pen shaft, cut a small nick to receive the top of the pen clip. Screw on the nylon nib protector and click housing onto the pen top.

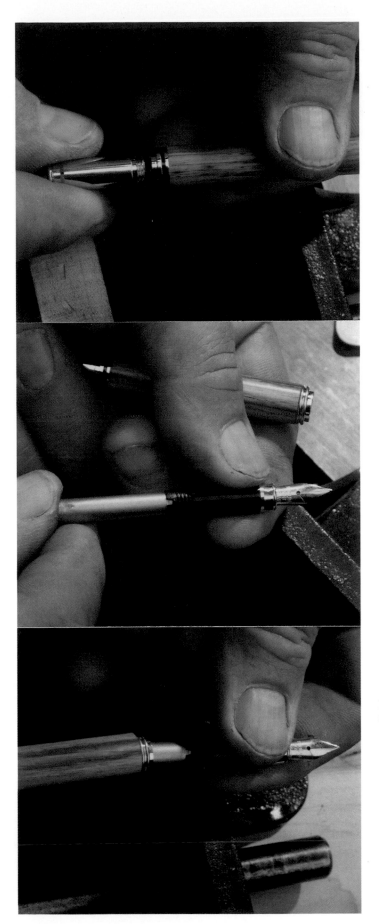

Now try the pen together and if there is movement between the body of the pen and the top ...

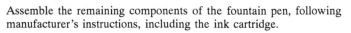

Assemble the remaining components of the fountain pen, following manufacturer's instructions, including the ink cartridge.

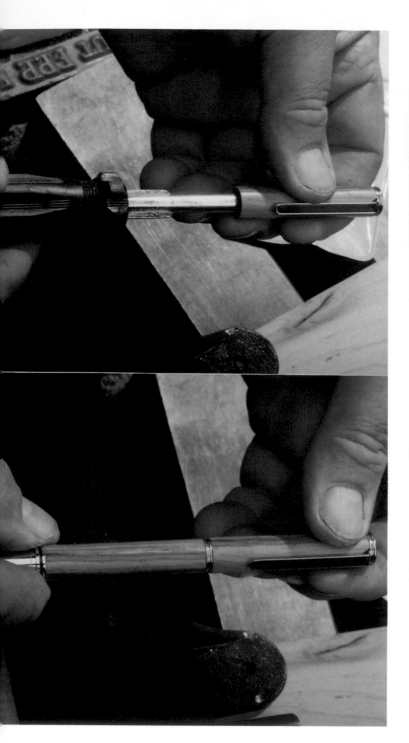

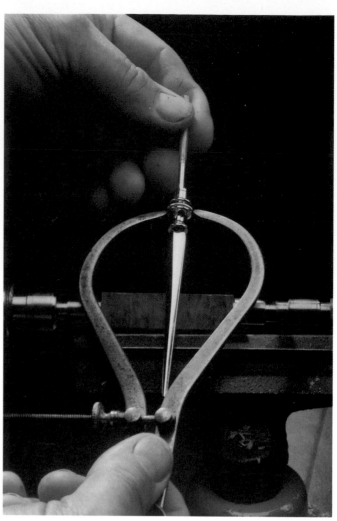

Next, we'll turn a handle for a letter opener. Measure the diameter of the collar with calipers.

... tighten down the nylon insert using a Phillips head screwdriver until you have a snug fit without side-to-side movement.

Note: as we saw with the Parker style fountain pen, not all fountain pens and ball pens need to have a groove cut for the clips. Some come with a flush fitting. So peruse the manufacturer's instructions and kits before assembling them.

The size of the end of the larger mandrel is exactly the right size.

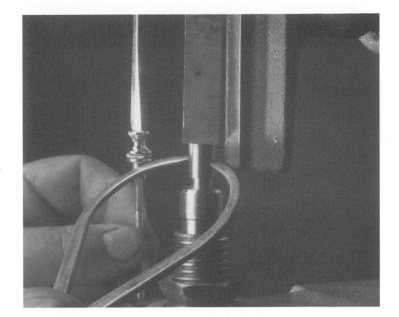

When turning a single piece of wood, fill the rest of the mandrel with spacers and extra wood.

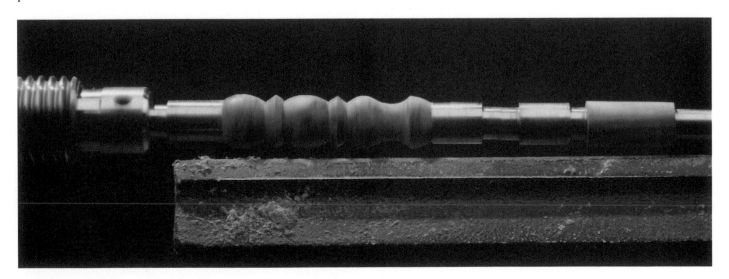

The material used for the letter opener handle is red resin impregnated burr wood. The design I have chosen is a simple one consisting of a ball, a bead, a ball, and a bead with a hollow and a taper coming up to the knife end as you can see in this photo.

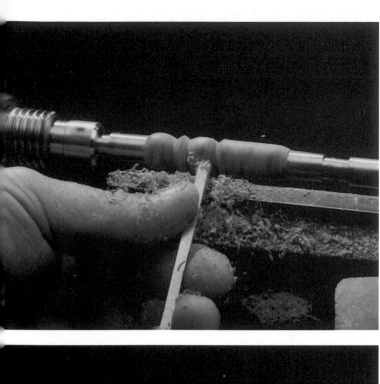

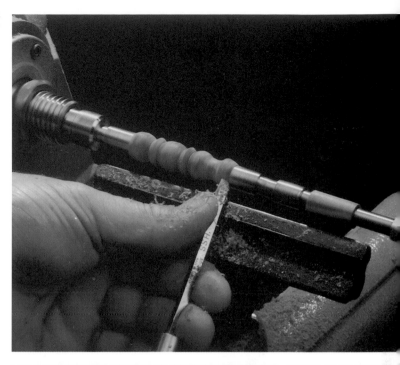

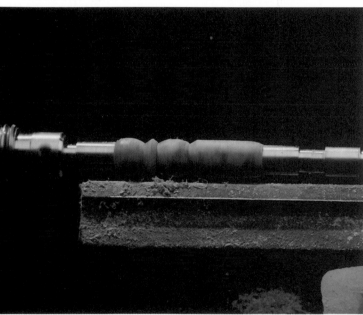

Follow the instructions given previously to form these shapes. With this material I found that the best tools to use are the beading and parting tool for the balls, coves, and beads and a small round nosed scraper for hollows and coves. With this material I have found you have to cut it with a gentler approach, otherwise chunks tend to pull out. Generally speaking, wood can be turned twice as fast. Do slow down for the best results when using this material. I love the look of this material and the manufacturer of this product seems to have the balance right, keeping the beauty of the burr — which would normally be flaky and crumbly — stablilized with resin so we can use it for small items. It is available in red, blue and yellow colors, all of which are very attractive.

Great care should be taken when sanding so as not to blunt over the nice sharp forms we have made.

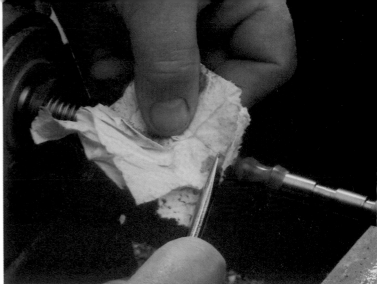

The edge of a screwdriver will help get your paper towel or soft cloth into tight areas for buffing.

Burnish with shavings.

Coat with both layers of stick polish and buff.

Adding the press fitting that will abut the blade to the finished handle.

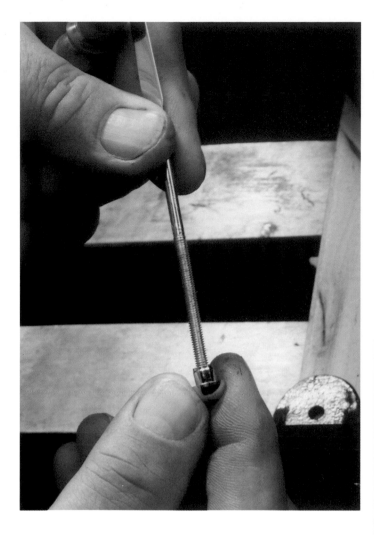

The end fitting is threaded and the screw end of the blade threads into it.

Adding the end fitting.

The finished letter opener.

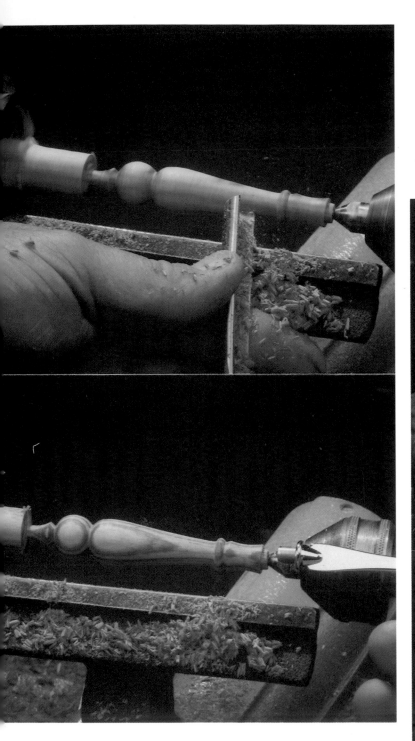

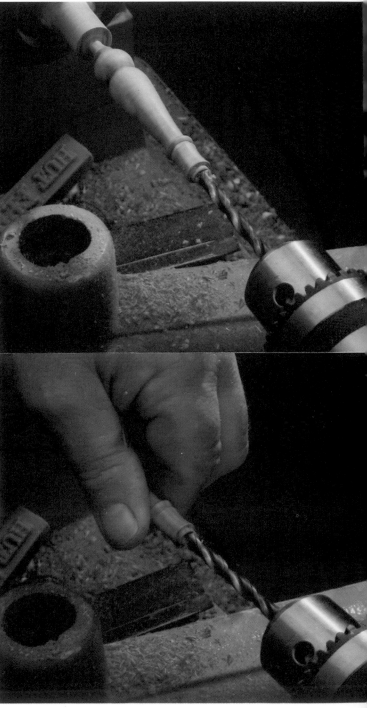

Using the techniques discussed previously, I am turning a letter opener handle out of tulip wood. A little bit of nice free hand turning. Making a traditional handled letter opener in tulip wood. The main tools used were the 1/2" special roughing gouge, 3/16" parting and beading tool, 3/8" skew chisel, and the 1/4" round nosed scraper.

When nearing the finished shape, check the diameter of the blade shank and carefully drill an appropriately sized hole in the end to the handle to receive the blade.

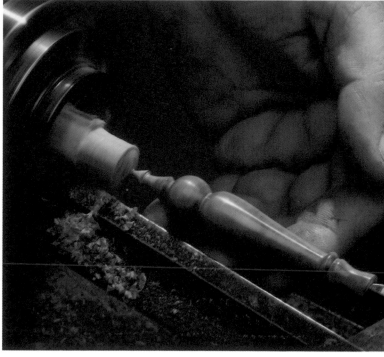

Gently insert the centre drive of the tail stock into the freshly drilled hole. Finish turning both ends of the handle on the lathe.

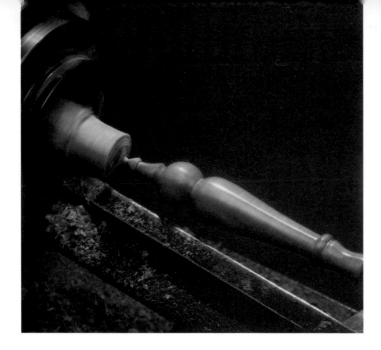

Bring the back end of the handle to a nice, delicate point which will free the handle from the scrap wood.

Now we'll make a small ladies pen for a purse.

Attach the blade, following manufacturer's instructions. The finished letter opener is an item of beauty.

For this project I'm using a miniature two pronged drive in the head stock. The hole in the wood is pre-drilled.

Turning the ladies purse pen following the methods explained previously. Allow yourself to be creative. Leave a narrow disk of waste wood at the far end of the handle for parting.

Sand and polish as before. Similar pens may be made with full sized pen refills and make nice gifts. They are inexpensive and quick to make. The polished pen handle.

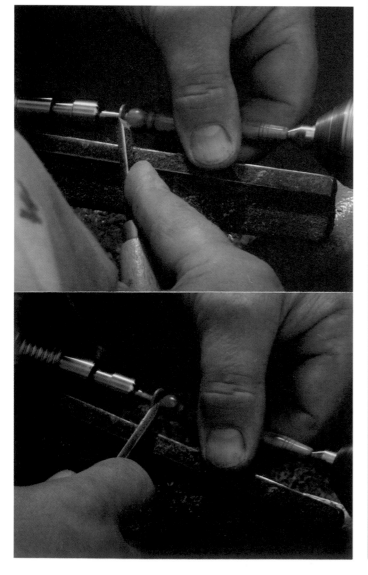

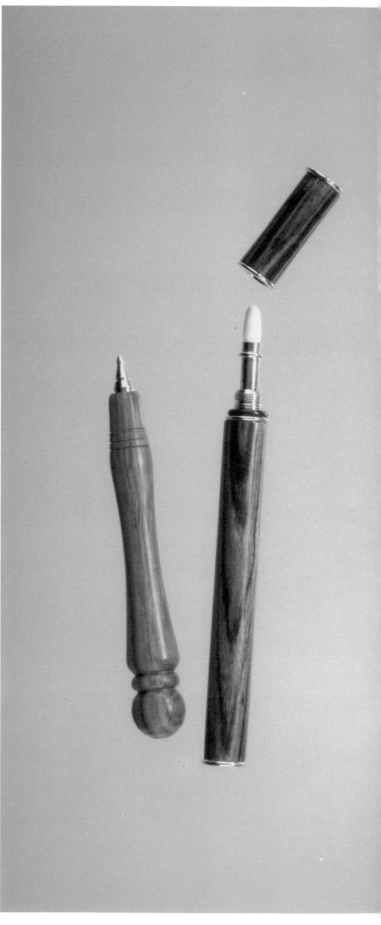

Parting the handle.

The assembled ladies pen along with the perfume dispenser.

GALLERY

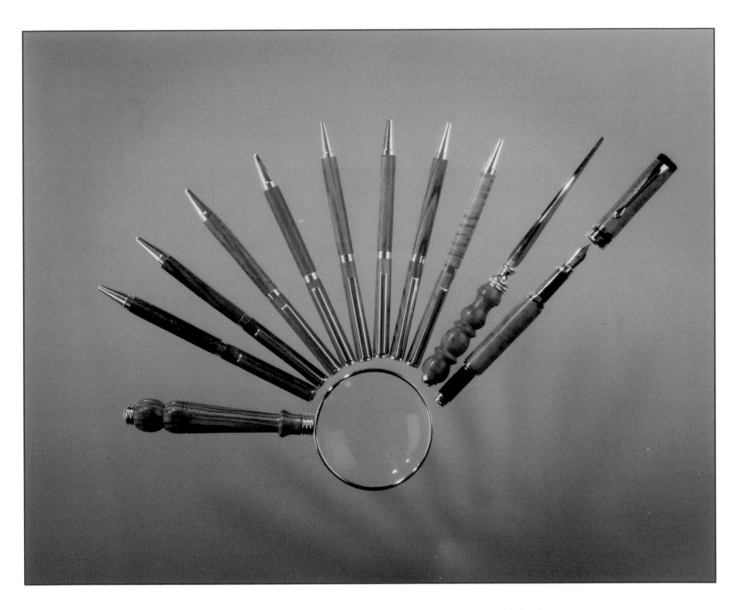

Desk top accessories, from letter openers to pens, turned for this book.

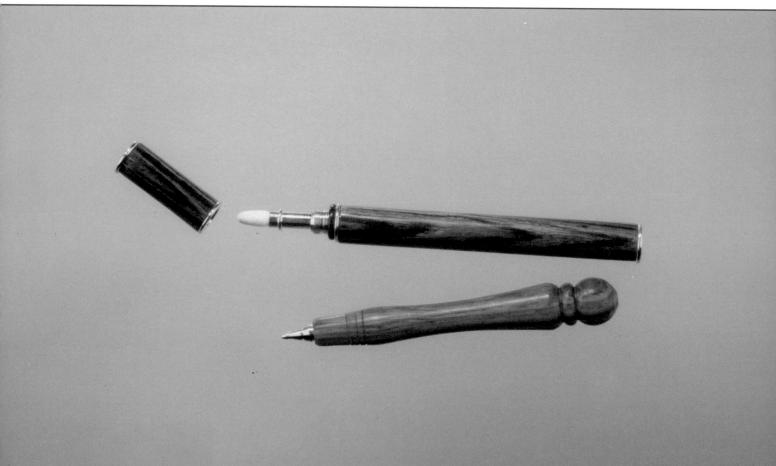

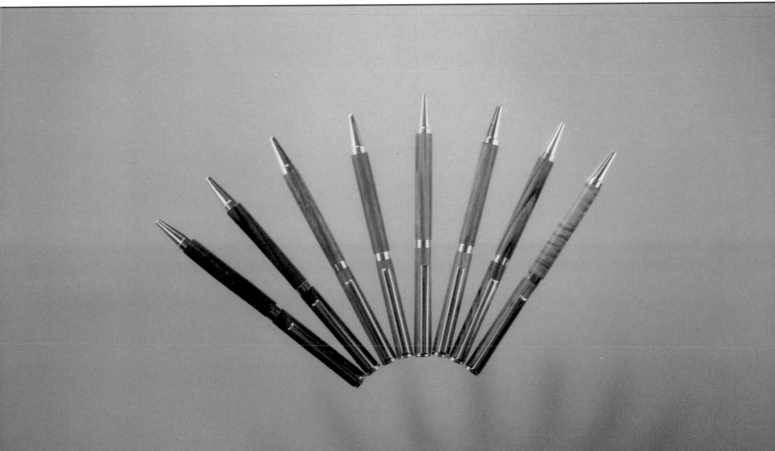

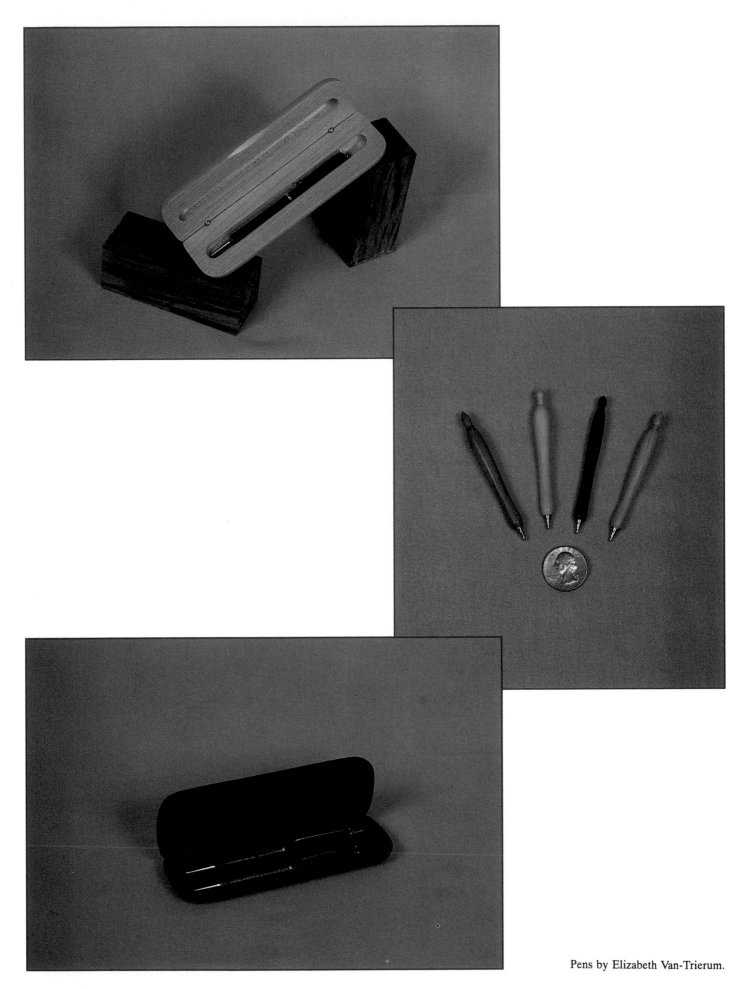

Pens by Elizabeth Van-Trierum.

Pens by Frank Finlater.

SUPPLIERS

Wood turners may contact the following suppliers to have their needs met:

Middlesex Woodcraft Centre
70 Woodend Green Road
Hayes
Middlesex
England
UB3 2SL
Phone: 0181 561 5885
Fax: 0181 561 5770
(Courses in wood turning, carving, and pyrography for beginners are offered here as well.)

John Boddy Fine Wood & Tool Store Ltd.
Riverside Sawmills
Boroughbridge
North Yorkshire
Y05 9LJ
Phone: 01423 322370
Fax: 01423 324334